NATIONAL
GEOGRAPHIC
KiDS

GO WiLD!
Lions

Margie Markarian

NATIONAL GEOGRAPHIC
WASHINGTON, D.C.

Lions are famous for their mighty ROARRRR!

It can be heard from five miles (8 km) away.
No wonder LIONS RULE!

Let's learn more about the king of beasts.

Beware of Cat!

Most lions live on the sunny savannas of Africa. They prowl and play in the dry grass.

Some lions live in a shady forest in India. They lurk and lounge among the tall trees.

Lion Lairs

Around 1900, there were about 200,000 African lions living in many places in Africa. Today, there are only about 20,000. Asiatic lions once roamed many parts of the Middle East and Asia. They have been rare there since the 1850s. These maps show where lions live now.

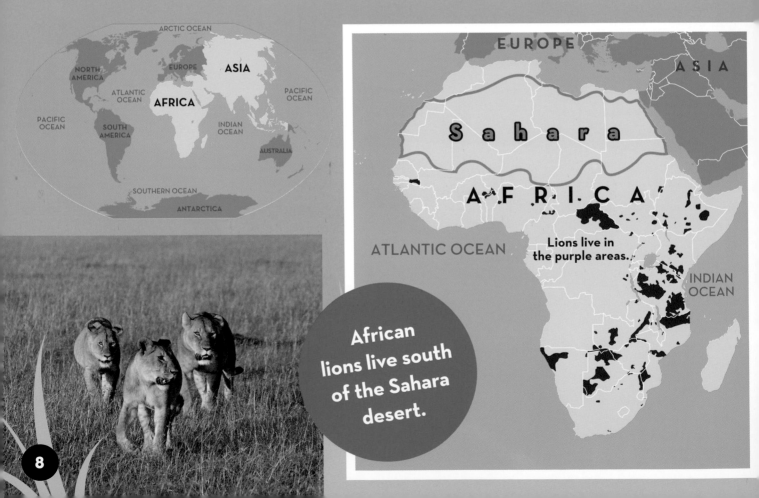

Lions live in the purple areas.

African lions live south of the Sahara desert.

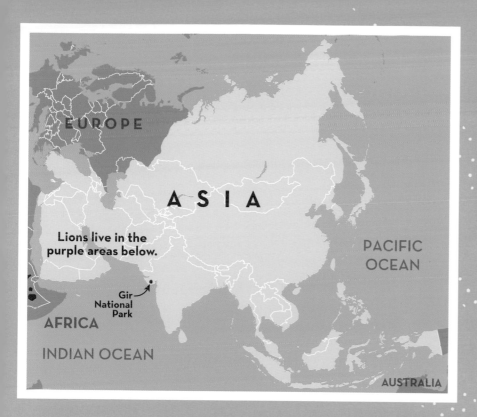

EUROPE

A S I A

Lions live in the purple areas below.

PACIFIC OCEAN

Gir National Park

AFRICA

INDIAN OCEAN

AUSTRALIA

Gir National Park in India is home to a small group of about 500 Asiatic lions.

Grand Stance

Lions are MAJESTIC.

Their long, strong bodies can stretch up to 10 feet (3 m) from head to tail tip. They typically weigh 270 to 420 pounds (122–190 kg) or more.

That's a lot of POUNCING POWER!

Big, Brawny Bodies

Lions are powerful predators. Their bodies are designed for hunting. Female lions do most of the hunting.

TAIL: Long tails provide balance for running and climbing.

FUR: Light golden brown fur helps lions blend in with their surroundings.

BACK LEGS: Long, muscular back legs help lions jump.

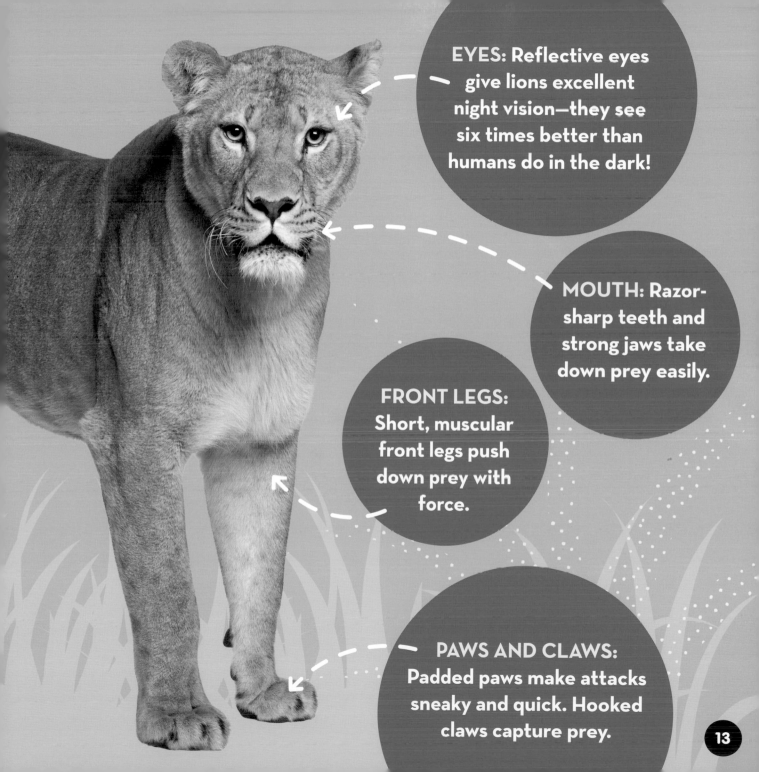

EYES: Reflective eyes give lions excellent night vision—they see six times better than humans do in the dark!

MOUTH: Razor-sharp teeth and strong jaws take down prey easily.

FRONT LEGS: Short, muscular front legs push down prey with force.

PAWS AND CLAWS: Padded paws make attacks sneaky and quick. Hooked claws capture prey.

Hairy Heads

Only adult male lions have manes. Their **FURRY FRINGE** is a sign of size, strength, and age.

Long, thick, dark manes attract female lions but warn enemies to **BACK OFF!**

Big Cats! Cool Cats!

Lions are one of four kinds of BIG, ROARING cats. Tigers, leopards, and jaguars are also BIG, ROARING cats.

TIGER

Tigers are the biggest big cat. They are the only big cats with stripes.

LEOPARD

Leopards and jaguars both have spots called rosettes.

Can you SPOT the difference? Leopard rosettes are rounder and closer together. Jaguar rosettes have bumpier edges and at least one dot in the middle.

JAGUAR

More Cool Cats!

Cheetah

Cheetahs are the world's fastest cats—they can run up to 70 miles an hour (113 km/h). That's as fast as a car drives on the highway. ZOOM!

Canada Lynx

This cool cat has extra-thick fur to handle frosty weather and supersize paws for walking on snow. *BRRRRR!*

Mountain Lion

Mountain lions aren't really lions! But they are members of the cat family. In fact, they are more closely related to pet cats than to lions.

Caracal

Pointy ears tipped with black hair give caracals an eerie look! BOO!

House Cat

A pet cat is much smaller than a lion, but it shares many traits—including a love of catnaps! *ZZZZZZ!*

Family Matters

Lions live in groups called prides. There can be as many as 40 lions in a pride. The average pride size is 15 lions.

The strongest male is the leader. He patrols the land with one, two, or three other males.

Females care for young lions and hunt together.

They all like to
NUDGE and
NUZZLE!

Meat Feast

Lions are CARNIVORES.
That means they eat
only meat.

Their favorite meals
are zebras, gazelles,
antelopes, wildebeests,
and warthogs.

Team Effort

Lions hunt as a team, often at night. Sometimes they search for and stalk prey. Other times, they watch and wait for prey to pass by.

Either way, the final chase is usually **FAST** and **FIERCE.**

Hello, Little Lion!

Baby lions are usually born in litters of two to four cubs. Cubs stay hidden in a den with their mom until they are ready to join the pride.

It's **SNUGGLY** and **CUDDLY** in the den!

At birth:
Newborns are
blind and helpless.
They weigh two
to three pounds
(0.9–1.4 kg).

6–8 weeks:
Time to meet the pride.
Hi, aunties! Hi, cousins!
You too, Dad!

3 months:
Mom's milk is still on the
menu, but tiny teeth are
ready to chomp meat.

1 year:
At 50 pounds
(22.7 kg), cubs are
ready for their
first hunts.

3-4 years:
All grown up! Male lions are
ready to leave home while most
females stay with the pride.

5-6 years:
Males are fully grown
and may challenge
other males for control
of the pride.

Hear Me ROAR and More!

Lions use many sounds to communicate.

Some are SOFT and LOW.

HUFF!

HUM!

PUFF!

GRUNT!

MOAN!

GROWL!

SNARL!

Some are LOUD and PROUD.

ROAR!

Of the approximately 40 species of wild cats, lions are the only ones that live in groups.

Tigers are the only cats bigger than lions.

There are small spines on a lion's tongue to help clean dirt from its fur and scrape meat off a bone.

It takes about two years for a lion to develop its deep roar.

Lions lick each other and rub heads to say hello and show affection.

Lions spend about 20 hours a day sleeping and lounging around.

The spots around a lion's whiskers create a pattern that's special to each lion.

Rumble of Trouble

Lions are mighty, but their future is shaky. They need a lot of land to roam and prey to eat. But their habitat is shrinking as towns and villages grow.

When lions can't find prey, they may attack animals on farms and ranches. People sometimes strike back by harming lions. Trophy hunting is also a threat to lions.

Protecting Prides

Many people are looking out for lions.

They have found ways to prevent lions from attacking livestock. One way involves building special fences called living walls. They are made of sturdy chain link and thorny trees that quickly grow tall. Lions can't break through or climb them.

Another way people are helping lions is by tracking them with computerized mapping programs. Ranchers watch the map. When the map shows a pride moving to a place where cattle are grazing, the ranchers have time to move the cattle to a safer place.

Protecting Prides

People are setting aside more protected lands for lions. Five African countries have joined forces to link their nature reserves into one huge park. This makes it easier for lions to roam, find prey, and raise **CUTE CUBS.**

People are also making more laws against hunting lions.

Show Lions

Want to help lions?

You can start by writing a letter to a group that helps to save lions. Tell them how much you love lions, and thank them for all their hard work.

Your kindness and caring could inspire more good deeds for lions!

Mane Game

Lions aren't the only animals with manes. These animals have them, too!

Point to each as you say its name.

wildebeest

horse

giraffe

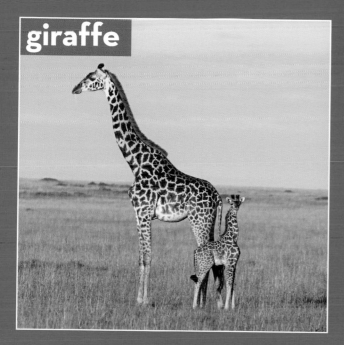

baboon

hyena

zebra

Want to build your child's enthusiasm for lions?

A great place to start is at a nearby zoo or animal park. Kids will be in awe of lions' huge size, loud roars, golden coats, and interactions with other lions. Watching online videos is another option if you can't visit a zoo. There are many amazing videos and articles about lions on the National Geographic Kids website at natgeokids.com.

Here are some other activities for you and your child to do together.

 ## Make a Mask! Hear Me Roar! Watch Me Pounce!
(Craft and Movement)

MATERIALS: a paper plate, markers, red and brown construction paper, brown yarn, scissors, glue, and a hole punch

INSTRUCTIONS: Invite your child to color the inner circle of the plate (the lion's face) yellow or gold and the outer rim (the lion's mane) brown. Help your child make cuts around the rim of the plate toward the center to give the mane its fringe. Then cut holes where the eyes should be. Next, use the construction paper to draw and then cut shapes for the mouth (a red oval), nose (a brown circle) and brows (two brown arches). Glue these pieces to the lion's face. Then cut six pieces of yarn to about three inches (8 cm) long and glue half the pieces to each side of the mouth to make whiskers. Punch a small hole on each side of the plate, pull a piece of yarn through each, and knot. Tie the strings together behind your child's head. Now your child is ready for a RIP-ROARING time prowling, pouncing, crawling, climbing, jumping, and stretching like a lion!

Animal Adventure Time!
(Observe, Record, Count, Graph)

Go on an animal adventure in your neighborhood or park. Bring along a notebook and have your child categorize and tally all the different types of animals they see—dogs, cats, rabbits, squirrels, chipmunks, birds, swans, geese, ducks, bees, ants, bugs, and more. Then have them create a colorful chart to display the final count.

 ## A Puzzle to Paw Over!
(Memory and Attention to Detail)

Help your child find a big picture of a lion's face online and print out two copies. Turn one of the pictures over and work with your child to draw puzzle-like shapes with a pencil. (Square puzzle pieces will also work well.) Guide your child to cut carefully along the lines. Now you are ready to turn the pieces over and let your child put together the puzzle, using the extra copy of the lion's picture as a reference.

 ## Lions in Everyday Life
(Research and Discussion)

Make a game of identifying lions used in books, movies, businesses, and pop culture! Start by doing online research; observing billboards, buildings, and statues; or be on the lookout while watching TV. Talk about some of the possible reasons why lions are used in these ways—strength, courage, power, majesty. These well-known lions can get the conversation rolling: characters in *The Wizard of Oz* and *The Lion King*; the lion statues in front of the New York Public Library; and the constellation Leo the Lion.

 ## Lion-Themed Poem
(Writing)

Introduce your child to poetry by having them write an acrostic poem about lions. Acrostic poems are simple poems that use all the letters in a topic word to create short descriptive sentences or phrases about the topic word.

Example:
CUB
C is for being *cute* and *cuddly*.
U is for *understanding* that lions need help.
B is for getting *bigger* every day!

GLOSSARY

carnivores: animals that eat only meat

cub: a baby lion

den: a hidden place in the bushes or a cave

habitat: an animal's natural home

livestock: animals such as cattle, goats, and chickens that are raised on a farm or ranch for food (meat, milk, cheese, eggs), clothes (wool, leather), and/or money

predators: animals that hunt and eat other animals for food

prey: animals that are hunted and eaten by other animals

pride: a group of lions that live together

reserve: a protected area of land or water

savanna: a large flat area of grassy land with very few trees

stalk: to sneakily follow something to catch it

For Dad, who loved watching animal shows and sharing fun animal facts —M.M.

AD=Adobe Stock; GI=Getty Images

Cover, Amanda Stronza/500px/GI; Back cover, Eric Isselee/Shutterstock; 1, Sandeep/AD; 5, gator/AD; 6 (UP LE), MaggyMeyer/iStock; 6 (LO RT), Michele Burgess/Alamy Stock Photo; 7 (UP), kuntalpaul/iStock/GI; 7 (LO RT), EMPPhotography/iStock/GI; 8, Pedro Helder Pinheiro/Shutterstock; 9, Kshitij30/Shutterstock; 10-11, weicool/Shutterstock; 12-13, Eric Isselée/AD; 14 (LO LE), shaunwilkinson/AD; 14-15, Eric Isselee/Shutterstock; 15 (UP RT), Laura Hedien/GI; 16 (LE), Colette/AD; 16 (RT), Engdao/AD; 17 (UP), Brian/AD; 17 (UP LE), mimagephotography/Shutterstock; 17 (LO RT), veneratio/AD; 17 (LO LE), worldswildlifewonders/Shutterstock; 18 (UP), Winfried Wisniewski/GI; 18 (LO), janstria/AD; 19 (UP LE), Rebius/Shutterstock; 19 (CTR RT), Ingo Arndt/Minden Pictures; 19 (LO LE), Alexandra/AD; 20, David Keith Jones/Alamy Stock Photo; 21 (UP LE), Paul Souders/GI; 21 (LO RT), Klein & Hubert/Nature Picture Library; 22-23, Anup Shah/GI; 24-25, Roy Toft/National Geographic Image Collection; 26, Paul Souders/GI; 27, stuporter/AD; 28 (CTR LE), Anup Shah/Nature Picture Library; 28 (UP), Anup Shah/GI; 28 (CTR RT), Heinrich van den Berg/GI; 29 (UP LE), Paul Souders/GI; 29 (LO CTR), Paul & Paveena Mckenzie/GI; 29 (UP RT), Ozkan Ozmen/GI; 30 (LE), Jami Tarris/GI; 30 (RT), JHVEPhoto/iStock/GI; 31 (UP), Derrick Neill/AD; 31 (RT), Štepán Kápl/AD; 32-33, Anup Shah/GI; 34, manfredstutz/Shutterstock; 35, brittak/GI; 36, African People & Wildlife/Felipe Rodriguez; 37, Sebastian Kennerknecht/Minden Pictures; 38-39, fusebulb/AD; 41 (UP LE), szefei/Shutterstock; 41 (UP RT), Isabel Pavia/GI; 41 (LO), elenarostunova/AD; 42 (LE), Erni/AD; 42 (RT), callipso88/AD; 43 (UP LE), Marie/AD; 43 (UP RT), Milan/AD; 43 (LO LE), Bruce/AD; 43 (LO RT), Ehrman Photographic/Shutterstock

Published by National Geographic Partners, LLC, Washington, DC 20036.

Copyright © 2023 National Geographic Partners, LLC. All rights reserved. Reproduction of the whole or any part of the contents without written permission from the publisher is prohibited.

NATIONAL GEOGRAPHIC and Yellow Border Design are trademarks of the National Geographic Society, used under license.

Designed by Kathryn Robbins

Library of Congress Cataloging-in-Publication Data
Names: Markarian, Margie, author.
Title: Lions / Margie Markarian.
Description: Washington, D.C. : National Geographic Kids, 2023. | Series: Go wild! | Audience: Ages 6-8 | Audience: Grades 2-3
Identifiers: LCCN 2022003537 (print) | LCCN 2022003538 (ebook) | ISBN 9781426373541 (hardcover) | ISBN 9781426373794 (library binding) | ISBN 9781426373855 (ebook)
Subjects: LCSH: Lion--Juvenile literature.
Classification: LCC QL737.C23 M267 2023 (print) | LCC QL737.C23 (ebook) | DDC 599.757--dc23/eng/20220202
LC record available at https://lccn.loc.gov/2022003537
LC ebook record available at https://lccn.loc.gov/2022003538

The author and publisher wish to acknowledge the expert review of this book by Jennifer Robertson, big cat keeper, Philadelphia Zoo; and the National Geographic book team: Shelby Lees, senior editor; Christina Sauer, associate editor; Colin Wheeler, photo editor; Mike McNey, senior cartographer; Alix Inchausti, senior production editor; and Gus Tello, designer.

Printed in Hong Kong
22/PPHK/1